THE PURPOSE
MAP

How to Have the Life You're Not Living

ERIC THOMAS

THE PURPOSE
MAP

To Latonyu,
Your best life
awaits you.

Sincerely,
Eric Thomas

TABLE OF CONTENTS

PART I
THE PRINCIPLES

1.1 The Solution To A Problem

"The two most important days in your life are the day you are born and the day you find out why."

-- Mark Twain

I peered around every corner and stuck my head out of every doorway before stepping into the hallway. I knew hiding was futile, but I would be cautious and attempt to avoid him as long as possible. If I was lucky, I could get through the school day without running into him. I sighed at the thought. He was a shark roaming the vast cream-tiled hallways of the high school, taunting and tormenting those like me that didn't have the acceptance and protection of a group or a clique. He fed off of me every day. They called him "Big Mike." He was short for a 10th grader. He bopped from side to side, unnaturally, with his broad shoulders rounded and a bend in his tapered waist, as though he was trying to touch his knees. His arms were thick like branches on an old oak tree with veins crisscrossing his forearms. Whenever I saw him, I couldn't help a short chuckle because he walked like the silverback gorilla I saw at the zoo. He wore a permanent scowl. I don't think he was able to smile. He usually wanted money and this particular Tuesday was no different. He pinned me against the lockers, a collar in each of his vascular hands, while the heads of his two flunkies swiveled around looking for teachers and security.

"I forgot my lunch money this morning, but I know you got some." The stench of rotting teeth, mustard and sardines reminded me of how the landfill nearby smelled during July. I thought about biting his nose off. I would get beaten to a pulp, but he wouldn't have a nose anymore. A broad smile crossed my face.

"Somethin' funny, Thomas?" He insisted on calling me by my last name.

"I forgot my lunch money too," I said, struggling to disguise the sarcasm in my voice.

"Bring money or your lunch to the cafeteria. You understand?"

I nodded quickly and smiled again as I thought about biting his nose off. He shoved me hard against the locker and bopped away. The lunch bell rang, 12:15. I darted for the back stairwell. I could get to the pizza place and back before lunch was over and not see Big Mike. I guess he was thinking the same as he spotted me running down the back stairwell.

"Where you goin'? The cafeteria's behind you."

"I'm leavin'. Goin' home. I'm sick." I grabbed my stomach.

"If you don't gimme some money, yo ass bout to be sick fo' real."

I lurched like I was about to vomit.

"You throw up on me and I'll kick yo ass up and down these stairs." He looked me up and down like he had just discovered something disturbing about me. "Thomas, you're useless and good for nothin'."

Big Mike brushed past me like I was a condemned man, swinging at the end of a rope, kicking, jerking, fighting, to keep his awful words from strangling the light out of me. Each letter gathered into the space you never want words like that to reside, your heart. I stood in that stairwell paralyzed, my mind repeating his words in disbelief trying to discern if they were true or to dismiss them. The rest of the day all I could think about was, "you're useless and good for nothin'." I had been called dumb, fat, slow, fathead, but never, ever, had anyone called me useless and good for nothing. I wished he had just punched me, slapped me. That hurt would have passed in a few hours. "Sticks and stones can break your bones, but words can never hurt you…" unless you believe them. Then, they can destroy you. I guess I believed his words because they hurt like hell and I was on my way to destruction.

I couldn't wait till school let out. I had to go see her. She would know how to put me back together and end my suffering.

My right foot was touching the bottom step of the steps to the school as the echo of the end of school bell rang through the courtyard. I ran as fast as my thick legs would allow to the one place I knew I could find understanding, compassion and solace. I threw myself on the porch of Ms. Hattie. Growing up, Ms. Hattie was our neighbor and the wisest person I have ever known. I was strewn across her porch like leaves scattered by a winter wind when she pushed open the screen door.

"Boy, who chasin' you? You hear me talkin?" My mouth hung open, sucking in every molecule of air trying to douse my burning lungs. I could only look up at her, my eyes pleading for her to understand my silence. She sat down on her porch swing and hummed.

Finally, I said, "Ms. Hattie, am I useless? Am I good for nothin'?" The swing came to a quiet stop. She leaned forward; her silver hair woven into two thick braids laid obediently down the middle of her back. The wrinkles of wisdom and experience accented her almond skin. Her lips curled up into a warm and loving smile.

She said, "Baby, everything created is the solution to a problem." I felt an antidote to the poisonous words "useless and good for nothin'" trickling into my heart. I looked around and everything I saw confirmed her statement. The porch swing, the house, the door, the trees, the ants crawling beside me, all of it, everything I could see was a solution to a problem. Everything had meaning. Nothing was brought into existence by accident or happenstance, including me. I had a meaning, a purpose. I had a job to do. I wasn't useless and I wasn't good for nothin'.

I sat upright, the biggest smile spreading across my face and into my body. My hands trembled. A surge of energy and excitement was racing through my veins. Ms. Hattie had cured me. She looked down at me glowing, smiling proudly, and fully aware of the inspiration she had impressed upon me. Ms. Hattie unconsciously brushed off her apron and stood up, knowing there was one thing left to complete my recovery.

"Boy, go inside and wash up. I'll fix you somethin' good. You look like you hadn't eaten since before you last closed your eyes."

I floated into the house filled with confidence, empty of doubt and unaware of something else her cure had awakened in me. It would challenge me and divert me from a comfortable path through life. It would be over 20 years before I would become aware of this something, this growing question. What was I was born to do?

ERIC THOMAS

1.2 The One Thing You Will Never Know

The thing you claim to know is the thing you are most ignorant of.

Nothing is ever forgotten. Over twenty years had passed since the day I was sprawled out on the porch of Ms. Hattie. Twenty years is a long time and a lot of memories get buried or pushed aside but nothing is forgotten. Nothing is ever truly forgotten.

And that growing question was not forgotten. It had continued to grow over those twenty plus years. I was now on the other side of 35 and each day becoming more aware of a fact. I wasn't living. I was just existing. I was a piece of paper, blown aimlessly through the streets and avenues of life by the winds of circumstance, my beliefs and the expectations of society. My dreams, goals and aspirations were in a pine box, buried under six feet of stress, fear, an empty, dead-end job, an unhealthy diet, 50 pounds of fat, two mortgages, and credit card payments. My life was a horror story and I was the writer with no idea how to rewrite the story. For so many years, I didn't even realize I was living a horror story.

I felt like a humanoid, having all the physical characteristics of a human being but my thoughts and beliefs weren't mine. I had been conditioned, programmed through suggestion, advice, direct instruction and the adults in my life as examples to get a job, to work for money so I could pay bills, save a little money, and get more stuff, all while unconsciously striving to be someone, anyone, but myself.

I was in disbelief, disappointed, unhappy, empty, frustrated, and angry. I had followed the program. I had taken the medicine prescribed by society that was supposed to make me happy and succeed. I was walking in the mantra. The prescription, the program, the mantra, go to school, get an education, so you can get a good job, work hard, build a career, save your money, invest, get married, buy a house, raise a family. I had done it the way it was supposed to be done and it had led me to frustration, emptiness, disappointment. I felt lied to. You could say I was living the American Dream and I should have been grateful. I had a home. I had a steady job, a little money in the bank and was raising two wonderful, healthy children. People in other countries risk their life and the lives of their family for a glimpse of this American Dream. I am grateful. I appreciate all I have but I was living the American Dream, not *my* dream. I wanted to live *my* dream, to discover what I was born to do.

There are thousands of books, classes, workshops, articles, courses, and more than a few movies, about finding your purpose and living a purposeful life. And I started reading many of those books about purpose, going to those workshops and watching those videos. In all I read, heard and studied, there was a recurring message, a consistent reference that has become a commonly held belief by most of society. Follow your passion or your passion will lead you to your purpose. And so, I did. I followed my passion. It's also said you have a special talent, we all do, and your purpose is usually found by exercising that talent or exercising the something you do very well. I took a hard look at myself and determined reading and writing always came easy to me. I struggled in math and science but I was always able to read and write on a level well beyond my age and grade and I enjoyed reading and writing. It became so clear. I was supposed to be a writer. My purpose in life was to be a writer. I *knew* it. But it's what I didn't know that would soon destroy the imagery of my purposeful life.

To *know* something equals being behind a locked door, a brick wall. I'll use losing my car keys to demonstrate this point. I was leaving to go to the store. I swept my hand across the counter to grab the keys and nothing. The edge of the countertop closest to the front door is where I always put my keys. I looked up, down and across the counter several times. As I'm standing there in disbelief a statement rolls through my head like a bowling ball, *I know I left those keys here on the counter last night.* For twenty minutes I walked around the house, in growing disbelief, always returning to the empty countertop and hearing that bowling ball roll through my head, *I know I left those keys here on the counter last night.* I stared at that cool, black and white marble countertop as though staring would make the keys appear. This continued for another fifteen minutes before I let go of that bowling ball. As long as that bowling ball was being tossed down the center lane of my mind I would never find the keys because I would not allow myself to expand my thinking of where they could be. I kept saying, I *know* I left those keys on the counter. My knowing closed the door, locked it, and built a brick wall to all the possible places the keys could be.

Once I let go of what I knew, I significantly improved the chances of finding the keys. And I found them in a place I never would have thought to look, on the nightstand beside my daughter's bed. She had been sick that day and when I got home, I went straight to her room, bypassing the kitchen. I never considered the keys could be in her room because I *knew* where I had left them. When you say I know this is my purpose in life or I know this is what I'm supposed to be doing with my life, you are closing the door, locking it and building a brick wall to the opportunities, possibilities, and solutions that can enrich your life more, bring more enjoyment, and more fulfillment.

This *knowing* prevented me from experiencing the life I imagined and intensely desired. Based on everything I read in books and articles along with listening to the thought leaders in purpose, I was supposed to become a writer. I enjoyed writing, I was passionate about writing, it came easily and I was good at it. Thoughts of being a writer had been in my head since high school. I *knew* I was supposed to be a writer and because I accepted this to be a fact, I unconsciously put limits on myself, closed myself to opportunities and created restrictions. As in the example of looking for the keys, I *knew* where the keys should be which put limitations on where I looked and what I did to find the keys. I stopped thinking and asking. My mind closed instead of expanding. The same happened when I *knew* my purpose was to be a writer. The door to whatever else was available closed. Infinite became finite. I stopped asking the question, "What else would I like to do?" I stopped asking, "Is this what I want to do the rest of my life?" The questions that spur growth and evolution were eliminated. I stopped asking the inspiring, motivating, questions because I *knew*. To ask questions, to continue to seek, meant I was doubtful, unsure about my purpose and what I wanted to do with my life. That doubt and insecurity was exactly what I didn't want. That would have sent me back to the original question, what was I born to do, and I didn't want to go through that again, so I allowed myself to accept what I *knew*.

Knowing creates a sense of calm, comfort and security. Take your job, for example. Every pay period you know you're getting a paycheck. It's as certain as a sunrise. Knowing this enables you to make plans, purchases and do the things you enjoy, which is calming, comforting, and makes you feel secure. One day a coworker stops by your desk and says he heard the company is cutting back and will immediately start a round of layoffs. Suddenly, you don't know if you'll be getting a paycheck the next week. Calm, comfort, and security are replaced with chaos, anxiety, and insecurity. The car you own has started every day for the last three years and never even had a flat tire. But, in the past few weeks you've had to replace the battery, two tires, the air conditioner stopped working and you were stranded on the highway because it overheated. Suddenly, old reliable isn't reliable. Once again, calm, comfort, and security are replaced with chaos, anxiety, and insecurity.

Worrying if you'll have a job the next week or worrying if your car will start the next morning destroys that sense of calm, comfort, and security. Because you're uncomfortable and anxious, you're open to other options and opportunities. Perhaps you were offered to move to another department, or a friend told you a similar position was available at their company and they could get you in. You declined because you knew your paycheck would be available. You knew the people at work, you knew the environment, the route to work, the expectations of the job, the expectations of the company. With your car, maybe you were asked by a friend if you wanted to sell the car. You declined because you knew the car was reliable, you knew it would serve you for many more years to come. You were in that calm, comfortable, secure feeling. You would not have seen, been aware, been open to the options and opportunities to move to another position or get another vehicle because *knowing* had you in a place of calm, comfort, and security.

Knowing my purpose was to be a writer created this aura of calm, comfort, and security. But knowing also made me single-minded and restricted my imagination. I delved into writing for a couple of years. Over those years I discovered I really enjoyed writing but I didn't want to spend my life as a writer. New ideas and topics to write about became difficult to cultivate. The material I was putting out didn't interest me as before. Words on paper weren't conveying my thoughts, ideas and opinions as powerfully as I wanted. Sitting behind a keyboard spitting out stories was no longer putting a big fat grin on my heart. I went from knowing I was meant to be a writer to simply believing. This shift in perspective allowed me to again think and ask the questions that spur personal growth and evolution. what else would I like to do?" "Is this what I want to do the rest of my life?" Again asking these questions brought me to an awareness I wasn't activating all of me and therefore not being fulfilled. I overcame the number one fear of adults, public speaking, and began speaking which I have come to love more than writing. Speaking creates a direct connection to my audience. Seeing their expressions, feeling their energy, and hearing their thoughts instruct me to form ideas that perpetually move people from where they are to where they want to be.

Knowing also creates the need to be right. I'm in the grocery store one day. The frozen food aisle was crowded so I parked my cart at the end of the aisle and walked to the frozen section. As I'm putting the items in the shopping cart a lady walks up and says, "You have my cart." Immediately, I became defensive. She made a statement, an accusation. Instinctively, I felt the need to defend myself, to prove she was wrong. Now, had she said, "I believe you have my cart" or "I think that's my cart," I would have been open and understanding of why she thought I had her cart. It would have been a dialogue instead of a conflict.

I felt accused. There was a wave of energy fueling a desire to be *right*. It's the same when you *know* your purpose. Subconsciously, you have something to defend. You must show yourself and others your life is on the right track, you made the right decision, that you know what you're doing.

The feeling to be right took over me when my circle of friends and family found out I wanted to do more than write full time. The questions and challenges erupted. "What are you doing?", "But you were so sure?", "I think you're doing the wrong thing.", "Have you thought this through?" Each question pressed me to doubt then affirm, doubt then affirm. Each affirmation was me verbally demonstrating I know what I'm doing, I'm making the right decision, you'll see I'm right. I wanted to demonstrate to others I was right in my choice but there was a requirement to demonstrate to myself I was making the right choice. Thinking this way will keep you locked on a path that only serves your ego and not your Self. Leaning toward being right will instruct you to continue what you're doing even though you're not happy, growing and being fulfilled. It's never about being right. It's always about doing what is best for your Self and honoring your Self.

There are moments when you hear, see or experience something that catapults your thinking to an extraordinary level. It's like you're jogging and suddenly you're traveling at light speed. One of these light speed moments happened when my oldest brother and I were talking about some of the obstacles to creating a life you enjoy living. He looked at me seriously and said, "It will make a huge difference if you understand you don't know anything."

Feeling disrespected I said, "What do you mean I don't know anything?"

"You don't *know* anything," he replied emphatically.

We went back and forth, me feeling more disrespected and stupid with each exchange. It took me several days to accept, but in the end his message became my truth. This truth has humbled me, made it much easier to create who I want to become and increased the level of peace in my life.

Whenever you say, "I know," or someone says, "I know," there are two things to consider, the words being spoken and the intention behind the words. The intention usually is to persuade or affirm. Countless times I've heard a friend say, "I know she's the one for me" or "I know I found my soulmate." I've also heard it said more than a few times, "I know this is what I'm supposed to be doing" or "I know this is what I was meant to do." I'm not exempt. I've said the same or similar often. What I now accept is whenever I claim to know something, I place myself in a closed space where the options, ideas and opportunities to achieve my best life aren't able to reach me.

The humbling truth is I know nothing. You know nothing. No one knows anything. There are examples of this truth all around. Every day, somewhere in this country, a law enforcement official will hold a press conference, step to a podium and announce, "We have made an arrest in the case of ———. We have a suspect in custody and we're certain we have the person responsible for committing this crime." Years (and in too many instances, decades) later, it's determined the wrong person was arrested, convicted and sent to prison. With the abundance of technology and centuries of crime solving knowledge and techniques, you wonder how so many innocent people are wrongly convicted. It's because of *knowing*. When the authorities say they know they have the right suspect, what they're really saying is we're not open to the possibility we may be wrong. We're not entertaining any other options of how the crime was committed or if another person could be responsible. We are done investigating. They have closed the door, locked it, and built a brick wall to prevent new leads, new information, new evidence, new suspects, ever reaching them. Often, new information is intentionally not acknowledged and new witnesses ignored, all because the authorities have fallen into the calm, comfort, and security of *knowing*.

There isn't a moment where I don't present myself as Eric Thomas and respond to Eric Thomas. You could say I *know* my name is Eric Thomas. I make decisions and choices that lift me or lower me based on knowing I am Eric Thomas. But how do I *know* my name is Eric Thomas? I didn't name myself. I wasn't even out of my mother's womb when I was named. So, how do I *know* my name is Eric Thomas? I don't. How do I know my parents are my parents? I don't. Again, I can't say with certainty my parents are my parents. If someone approached me tomorrow with a certified birth certificate claiming they are my biological parents and they put me up for adoption when I was born, what could I say? I couldn't say they're wrong because I don't know. I was *told* who I am and who my parents are. It's true, I don't know, yet when I hear my name or speak my name, I respond and speak it with assuredness and conviction. In this area of my life, it serves me to walk in knowing. I don't want to walk around every moment of my life without the ability to identify with a name or a persona.

You don't know your name. You don't know who your parents are. So, how can you *know* your purpose? How can you *know* what you were born to do? You don't know. When it comes to purpose and what I was born to do, I have chosen not to walk in knowing. Just as you don't know your name or who your parents are, you don't know what your purpose is or what you were born to do. And anyone that tells you they know, or they can tell you your purpose is lying or misinformed. How can anyone, especially a stranger, tell you something about yourself you don't even know? There are indicators and signals and clues that will bring you closer and align you with experiences that fulfill you and bring you enormous joy but you can never know, just as you can never know why you were born the way you are or why you're good at dancing and everyone else in your family has two left feet. You may have an idea, an opinion, a strategy to find a purpose for your life, maybe even a belief, but you will never know. And how would you know? Is it written down somewhere in a book? When you find your purpose is the book revealed to you confirming you have found your purpose? When you find your purpose, are there fireworks along with a big congratulatory message, "congratulations Eric, you have found your purpose." Does God, the universe speak in a warm, deep voice, "Eric, you've done it. You've found your purpose. Now you can go on with your life."

Once you accept that you know nothing, your life will be infused with a freedom you have never experienced. There will be no more anxiety around searching, seeking, looking for this thing you were told you needed to discover. You can unshackle yourself from this innate thing which everyone touts will bring you happiness, give you cause to wake each morning, energized and grateful. I have the understanding knowing is not a requirement and I know nothing. This allows me to remain open and receptive to new information, knowledge which is the fodder for growth and to evolve. I live according to a set of beliefs. This is so wonderful because I can release a belief at the moment it no longer serves me. I have no attachment. New information, more understanding, more knowledge and wisdom are presented to you every second of every day so why would you ever want to allow yourself to be shackled to a claim of knowing something when you can be free to learn, grow and experience so much more just by letting go of knowing.

Why spend all this energy, time, emotion, money and resources seeking to know an unknown. Why not put your energy into pursuing what you can be sure of and that is what makes you happy and fulfills you? You don't need anyone or anything to tell you what thrills you. You don't need anyone or anything to tell you what moves you, what energizes you, what fulfills you, what you are grateful for. It doesn't matter what your purpose is. What matters is that you live with intention and purpose. Live with an insatiable desire to learn, grow and experience all the Universe has to offer. And learning how to live in that way is awaiting you on the next page.

ERIC THOMAS

1.3 You Can Have More Than One

Live with a purpose, not for a purpose.

Accepting that you don't know your purpose and can never know contradicts everything you've heard and been told. Your entire life you've been conditioned and programmed to believe it's your duty in life to know your purpose. That message has been seeded into your mind like a seed pushed into the soil. It took me months before I allowed myself to believe I didn't know my purpose in life and I could never know. This was also one of the most liberating beliefs. It shifted me from a mindset of looking and seeking to a mindset of creating. I wasn't a bystander anymore. I was an active player in my life. I was the star in a one-man play. This was empowering but also unnerving. It meant I was responsible for what I got or didn't get in life. That's a lot of responsibility to accept. To go from "God has a plan for you" or "something is guiding your footsteps" to Eric you're driving and totally responsible for getting yourself to the destination, was an alteration in my belief that sometimes kept me from sleeping.

I may not have known my purpose, but I still knew I had one. I had to have a purpose. That's what everyone said, it's what I read in all the popular books. I not only needed to find my purpose, but I also had *a* purpose. It was the one thing I was designed, created to do and I could find it by looking at the one thing I enjoyed doing the most. This required more self-examination so I would sit quietly and go into my mind to see what I enjoyed the most. If I could only do one thing what would that thing be? That's the question all the thought leaders and experts about purpose said I should ask. I spent weeks, months, years on this question which led me to ask another question, suppose I don't have one thing? Why am I limited to one? I'm a human being possessing the most powerful tool in the Universe, imagination. There is nothing I cannot conceive in my imagination. It is as infinite as the universe, yet here I am looking for a purpose, the one thing that is supposed to bring me happiness, joy and fulfillment. This mainstream message about having *a* purpose wasn't fitting me.

Even a tree has more than one thing it can do well. It has more than one purpose, more than one thing it was created to do. I don't believe anything has *a* purpose. We assign a purpose based on the value the thing provides to us. We say the purpose of a tree is to make paper products because that's what we deem most valuable and meaningful. To a squirrel a tree provides food, to a bird, shelter and the earth may see a tree as helping to keep soil from being washed away during heavy rain. Each entity has its own definition of the purpose for the tree, so how can it be said the tree has *a* purpose?

Dr. Martin Luther King was born to lead the civil rights movement. This statement is touted every year during his birthday celebration by the media, leaders and followers. It's like a footnote to his life. Leading the civil rights movement is assigned as his purpose, the one thing he was born for. Really? Suppose Dr. King decided to write poetry, be a schoolteacher, or simply work in a steel mill and raise a family. Would he have not lived up to his purpose? For many, his purpose was to be a leader, to his children it may have been to be a loving father and grandfather. To his wife, it may have been the husband to grow old with. To his friends, someone to laugh and joke with, someone who was loyal and compassionate. To his employer, an employee that could be counted on to do an excellent job, day in and day out.

Do you believe you were born for a purpose, born to do some specific thing? Let's say, one day you're driving to work. A car runs through a red light and rams the driver's side of your car. At impact, your head is slammed against the driver side window. You awake in a hospital. You don't know your name, you don't recognize your spouse, children, parents, friends. You don't even recall what you did that morning. The doctor says you have complete amnesia. What happens to that thing you were born to do? It's been lost to you. How do you get it back? Is your life meaningless now? Here's another scenario. For as long as you could remember, you've been told "you were born to be a musician." You played the piano and the saxophone throughout elementary and high school. Three classmates shared your love for music, y'all formed a quartet and played through college. After graduating you gave up music and took up sculpting. Does that mean you weren't "born to be a musician?"

It may not be said directly but it's implied in the wording and stated in the intention. When I was in school the one question I would get from my guidance counselor, teachers, and well-meaning adults was "Eric, what do you like to do?" Immediately, my mind would flip through all the things I liked to do. I was a kid, full of energy and imagination, bursting with things I loved to do. And these people were trying to narrow me down to one. Why just one?

What's the *one* thing you want to do more than anything else? What do you want to do when you grow up? And God forbid you have more than one thing or interest. "Something's wrong with this child, he doesn't know what he wants to do when he grows up." It gets worse if you're in college approaching your junior year and you don't have a major or know what you want to do. You're "lost," "confused," "need to grow up." This oneness, singularity, is reinforced even more after college. You've graduated and now you're an "adult." You're supposed to have a career path. You're not sure but you feel obligated to pick one. Spend most of your life on that career path and you're likely rewarded with pay raises, promotions, credibility, tenure, respect. Move to a new career path and you must start at the bottom rung and work your way up. A deterrent to becoming your best Self.

This message that everyone has *a* purpose has been accepted and spread to the masses as a truth. Its effect is a chain around your neck binding you to a life of seeking, searching, and never living. I was trapped by this message for decades. I am a being with an infinite capacity to imagine and create, yet I am being programmed, taught, conditioned to settle on a *single* meaning for my life. Just like you can have more than one lover, one spouse, one home, one career, you can have more than one purpose. And you can change it as often as you change your underwear.

Since I understood I didn't know my purpose, would never know it and had no purpose, I had the freedom to be anything and try anything. I could be and do whatever my Spirit, my Self desired. I could try it, not like it, and move to the next thing. I wasn't stuck seeking this one thing so incredible I would spend the rest of my life doing it. It was like dating. I could try different tones, education levels, cultures, shapes, sizes, and not be bound to finding the one. If the one appeared I could spend my life in that experience and if it didn't, I would spend the rest of my life enjoying the infinite experiences with the joy and happiness each new experience would bring. I couldn't be let down or disappointed because I wasn't looking for any one thing. I wasn't expecting the one thing to appear. I was free to be and let my *Self* rule. I thoroughly enjoy speaking and writing but if my voice were diminished to a whisper and my fingers stiffened, then I will find another outlet, a new meaning to rise smiling, and bursting with energy.

The same applies to you. Don't assign yourself to one thing. Do one thing, then another, then another, and another, and if you enjoy them all, then do them all, and if you enjoy none, then part ways and seek a new experience. But know you are not looking for one thing to captivate you. This is not a requirement. The only requirement is for you to be happy and eager for the next day and if one thing does this for you, wonderful. If not, join me in building a stable and filling it with all the activities you love. And you will find the journey toward your final day an immeasurable joy renewed with each sunrise. You are too incredible of a being to have your Self asphyxiated by walking a singular path in life. The ideal life you desire awaits you. You already have the designs for this life. Now, all you need do is apply the infinite creative capacity of God within you.

1.4 Create

"You have to create your life. You have to carve it, like a sculpture."

— William Shatner

I hate to misplace or lose anything. Losing or misplacing my keys, wallet, sunglasses means I must look for them and I hate looking for anything. I'll spend some time looking for it but how much time is determined by how much it cost. I'd rather go out and buy another and avoid spending the time and the frustration spent looking for it. Looking for something ties up your mind, your focus, your energy. During the time you're looking for it, you're totally invested. Nothing else matters except what you're looking for. You're anxious, irritable, frustrated and tired mentally from going over and over in your head where it could be. Wouldn't it be so much easier to just buy another one? It would, but sometimes the thing you're looking for can't be purchased.

All of my adult life I've heard the message or been given the advice, "you need to find your purpose." The message spread through me during my late 30s and for the next several years I was all about "finding my purpose." Looking. Seeking. Finding. I tried all the strategies, steps, secrets but I couldn't seem to find this thing called purpose. I already mentioned how I hate looking for anything. *Finding* my purpose made me anxious, irritable and frustrated. It all felt like work, another job, another task I had to do. This was supposed to be a fun, exciting journey of discovery. I was not having fun.

In chapter two I mentioned I came to understand you will never *know* your purpose. So, I had to ask myself, if I don't know what my purpose is how can I find it? How are you going to find something and you don't know what you're looking for? At least if you're looking for your keys, you'll know you've found the keys because you knew what you were looking for.

You would recognize the keys when you found them. Talking about purpose, you don't know your purpose, yet you're supposed to know it when you find it. It just didn't make sense.

To truly grow you must always be willing to let go of what you *know*. If society has programmed everyone to go left, is it ludicrous to let go of that programming and consider going right? I was tiring of following the "you need to find your purpose," crowd. Instead of *finding*, why not create? Create. Saying the word excites feelings of strength, power, responsibility, authority. It makes you feel like a God. I feel the presence of God every time the letters roll off my lips. Create.

When you create something, it comes from you. It's not someone else's idea or plan, it's yours. Your idea, your thought. You have the blueprint, the design, the intimate details. You know how it will look, feel, smell, act, the impact it will have on others. Because it came from you it will be what you desire as you desired. You cannot be disappointed. You know all of this because it is of your mind, your creation. If a car, plane, skyscraper, ocean, galaxy, planet, can be created, why not a purpose? Why can't you sit down with your Self and create meaning, fulfillment and happiness in your life?

You are a creative machine. All you do is create, every second of every day. So why would you ever consider *finding* something when you have the power to create whatever you desire? Why *find* a purpose for your life when you can *create* a purpose for your life? To create is powerful. There's no more I can't have or can't do because this person won't let me or that person won't help me. There's no more I can't because of this circumstance or that circumstance. The responsibility of your life is on your shoulders and that may be too much for you to accept. So, you look for an authority, someone or something you can give power over you. You want this person or thing you have given power over you to tell you what you *must* to do to have the life you want. You spend enormous amounts of time, energy, money and emotion looking for someone's strategy, a 10-step program. Now you have something you can follow and when you don't get the desired results, you point the finger at the program, the person, the idea, the advice, as the reason for your disappointing results. Making someone else responsible is so worth all the time, energy, money and emotion. You're off the hook. You simply say his strategy didn't work or her method wasn't a fit for me. Creating is like baking a cake, you have all the ingredients but if the cake isn't good you can't blame it on the butter, eggs or flour. Very few know how to create the life they desire and so, very few live their best life. Are you ready for the responsibility, freedom and power of a creator? Do you want to know how to create?

Remember as a child how free you were at play? There were no rules to limit or restrict you. A rock could be a truck traveling down the highway. A leaf in a puddle could be a boat traveling on the ocean. A folded piece of paper could be a unicorn. A twig could be an airplane. As a child, I would often be a New York City subway conductor, rolling and swaying along the gleaming rails braided upon the landscape of the city.

My hips swayed, torso jolted and heaved as I chugged down the sidewalk, arms churning, tongue clicking, voice squealing at the right pitch, as I leaned into a sharp curve along the imaginary rails. As a child, I wasn't afraid, ashamed or embarrassed to express my imagination. I didn't have a care who saw me chugging down the sidewalk. But as an adult you don't feel comfortable sharing, expressing what your imagination holds. You're probably too ashamed to openly daydream anymore.

You create your purpose by listening to your Self. Your Self is always communicating with you, but you rarely listen. You ignore its signals, words, attempts to get your attention. Your Self is a stepchild who you disrespect and only when you are the most frustrated, disgruntled, empty, disappointed, and unhappy do you allow its whispers of advice and guidance to enter and counsel you. Your Self is always stating the following truths, there is nothing you cannot have. There is nothing you cannot do. There is nothing you cannot be. Your life would be incredible if only you would listen and take action on the desires of your Self.

The Self is the real you. It is your Soul, your Spirit. It knows intuitively what it wants to experience and learn in this life. The problem is your parents and the world have programmed you to chase jobs, careers, homes, money, promotions, cars, clothes, status, vacations, degrees, influence and every other shiny object. You will give your entire life to a struggle to acquire these things only to realize in the end they are empty objects that could never fulfill you. To keep you conscious of what is important, ask yourself these three questions periodically or at the start of your day. What do I want to do? What do I want to be? What do I want to have? Put these questions to your Self, to your Soul, to your Spirit. What would you love to do? What would you love to be? What would you love to have? And when the answers come, create a life where you can do what you want to do, be what you want to be and have what you want to have. Purposeful living is about *creating*, not finding.

Do you remember how real the things in your imagination were when you were a child? When I imagined I was a subway conductor, I clearly envisioned myself standing in the cab sliding the stainless steel, t-shaped throttle forward, applying the brakes, feeling the wind and snow on my face as I slid open the cab window to watch the passengers enter and exit the train. It was as real to me as your reflection in the mirror. Now imagine what you want to do, what you want to be and what you want to have with that same clarity, with that same enthusiasm, that same adamant belief. Allow yourself to feel the excitement, happiness, joy and freedom attached to what you want to be, do and have. In your imagination, there are no rules, no boundaries. Anything can be conceived and developed with no worry or thought of *how*. You operate as God. This is the process of creating.

You are your purpose and your purpose is manifested within whatever you create. If you want to create a life where you lounge on the beach, watching sunsets and drowning in margaritas, then you have created your purpose. There is purpose in whatever you create because you are the creator. Who has the authority to say you were born to do more than lay out on the beach? Who is qualified to say you're wasting your life and you were born to do more? If you create the life you desire, you won't have the burden and anxiety of finding your purpose. But how do you know what you want to create?

1.5 It's Not Passion

"Frustration is fuel that can lead to the development of an innovative and useful idea."

— Marley Dias

The power to create is enormously empowering, encouraging and freeing. But what will you create and how will you determine what to create? Yes, you want to create a happier, more enriching, meaningful life, but how do you determine what is important, what is meaningful to you? Trial and error? Suggestions from friends? The old-fashioned way, do what you're good at, do what you love? But suppose you have a talent for more than one thing, or you have a love for more than one thing. I fall into this category. I have a talent for writing and a talent for speaking. I love studying and writing about beliefs and how they shape every single choice and decision. I love speaking. I love mentoring and guiding people to their best life. Having to choose one path and devote my life to it isn't an option for me. For years I traveled the "passion will lead you to your purpose" road. The more I traveled that road, the more I found myself anxious, unhappy and disappointed with how my life was unfolding. I could never have imagined a speech I was giving for a Toastmasters contest that mentioned Josephine Cochran, Donald Fisher, and Samuel Morse would open my eyes to what I wanted to do with my life.

Josephine Cochran was a woman with plenty of time and money who enjoyed hosting dinner parties for her socialite friends. Josephine Cochran invented the dishwasher. Her incentive wasn't money, she had plenty of that. She had a good heart but making the lives of her servants better wasn't her primary motive. She certainly didn't invent the dishwasher to save her time cleaning up after dinner. Why would a woman of means invent a dishwasher?

In 1969, Donald Fisher was a San Francisco real estate developer. Mr. Fisher spent a lot of time going from one department store to another looking for jeans that would fit his lanky body. He never found a pair of jeans that would fit him but he did come up with an idea that would transform the retail and fashion industries by creating The Gap. What would cause an established real estate developer to move into the fashion and retail industry, areas where he had absolutely no experience or knowledge?

Samuel Morse graduated from Yale in 1810 and pursued a career as a painter. He went to England to study art and in 1815 returned to America and set up a studio in Boston. He traveled much of the East Coast painting portraits of notable people. In 1825, while away working on a portrait, he got word his wife was very ill after giving birth to their third child. By the time he arrived home she had died and already been buried. Ten years later he was developing the telegraph along with what came to be known as Morse Code. What would cause an established painter to cross over into an area where he had no experience, knowledge or resources and persist to develop a technology that didn't exist?

None of these people had a talent or a gift for the idea they created and developed. They *had no passion* to be inventors or entrepreneurs. Inventions and entrepreneurship weren't on the path they were traveling through life. Yet, something energized them to learn, study, create and develop what did not exist. And *passion* wasn't the primary energy source.

In that speech I wrote for the Toastmasters International Speech Contest was an answer to a question I had been asking myself since that afternoon on Ms. Hattie's porch, *what was I born to do?* The speech referenced Samuel Morse, Josephine Cochran, and Donald Fisher and their inventions and accomplishments. None of these people set out to do what they did. The old storyline about *passion will lead you to your purpose*, wasn't in their story. Something had directed these people and it wasn't passion. And this thing was also directing me. I just didn't know what *it* was until I began to learn the speech. I rehearsed each line, each movement, each facial expression, the tone, for days, weeks, and months. As I rehearsed, a message within the speech became overwhelmingly clear, passion alone would never lead me to anything just as passion had not led these people to their greatest accomplishments and inventions.

Passion is considered a key ingredient to succeeding simply because we have accepted *your passion will lead you to your purpose* and similar beliefs as *the* truth. There is some truth to the belief but it is not *the* truth. Think about it, what really brings meaning and happiness to your life? It's not passion. You don't see people running around talking about how happy they are because they have a passion. Have you ever said, I have a wonderful life because I'm passionate about helping people, or my life has meaning because I'm passionate about my career? Probably not.

Passion is like a volcano erupting. It's big, noisy, gets a lot of attention and the surrounding landscape is changed forever. Passion is volatile. Passion is spontaneous. It moves you to act without a lot of thought or consideration. Passion says *just do it*. You have a passion to paint so you run out and buy canvas, easels, brushes, paint, join an artist community and dive into the ocean of painting. Someone asks you, what do you want to paint," and after some thought you realize you have no idea what you want to paint. All you know is you're desperate to put something onto a canvas. This is the flaw of passion. Passion led you to move, act, do, but do what? What are you going to focus your time, energy, money, and emotion on?

Passion showed me my love for writing which expanded my heart to embrace speaking. But what am I going to write about? What am I going to speak about? How will I know what to focus my time, energy, money, and emotion on? Passion couldn't answer those questions for me. Passion told me to just do it but after years of just doing it, I realized I had no focus. It was like I was painting by throwing paint against a canvas. My words had no shape, no form. They moved no one to do anything. They were just words lying obediently on the paper. Passion had taken me as far as it could. Like me, you followed the *passion will lead you to your purpose* path because that is the message programmed into you and reiterated throughout your life. You stayed on the path because you didn't know what else to do and the thought leaders in the Purposeful Life industry never gave you a new message, an alternative. And like me, you remained unfulfilled, unhappy, and desiring to have the life you weren't living. Instead of looking for what energizes and excites you, perhaps you should look for what incenses you and aggravates you?

After years of aimless writing and speaking, *it* revealed itself in that speech for the Toastmasters International Speech Contest. It was frustration. Frustration was the ingredient I was missing. Actually, it was never missing, I just didn't recognize it and what it could do in my life. Frustration is a really misunderstood feeling. It's often mistaken for anger. Frustration can lead to anger but it's not anger. Frustration has been wrongly labeled as a negative feeling. When you're frustrated, you're short-tempered, impatient and probably not in a good mood. Frustration isn't about making you feel good. It wasn't designed to make you feel good. This is part of why it's misunderstood and considered a negative. And for this reason, frustration isn't as attractive as passion in the conversation around purpose.

When viewed in its proper perspective, frustration is an effective guide and is essential to having the life you're not living. Sir Edmund Hillary would never have summited Mt. Everest without his Sherpa, his guide, Tenzing Norgay. Sir Edmund would have plodded around Mt. Everest seeking a path to the top, his passion to climb and explore never waning, but he needed a guide to show him the way to the summit. He had the passion, but he didn't have the way. Frustration is the Sherpa, the guide. It is the way. Unlike passion, frustration is stable and deliberate. Frustration is a finger pointing out what irritates you. Frustration is like your social security number or your fingerprint. Your frustrations are unique to you. Experiences that grate your nerves go unnoticed by others.

My wife at the time and I were at a jazz festival and after one performance the host brought two children onto the stage to announce to the audience these children were lost and couldn't find their parents. The children were between 8-10. I couldn't understand how a parent could lose their child or allow their child to wander away from them during an outdoor concert spread over 20 acres with over 20,000 people and at night. I was appalled. My wife took it much further. It bothered her to where she said, "Let's go. I can't sit here and enjoy myself knowing those kids are lost and scared out of their minds. I wanna choke those so-called parents."

We witnessed the same experience. I was affected mildly and she was affected intensely. Not everything will frustrate others on the level it frustrates you. This is the identifying, guiding characteristic of frustration. The intense response of my wife indicated she has no tolerance for children being mistreated. I have seen her respond with similar intensity each time she witnessed a child is being mistreated. It's not a coincidence that she runs afterschool programs at a couple of elementary schools. She didn't know it but it was the quiet persistence of her frustration with children being mistreated that pointed out a space where she could develop a meaningful, happy, purposeful life and earn a very good living while doing it.

Frustration identifies the problem(s) you address or solve. You don't have to guess what inspires you or fulfills you. Now, you can ignore the frustration, which most people do, and remain unhappy but it will continue to appear to you, affect you and matter to you. Or you can acknowledge and accept the frustration. Listen to it. Feel it. Understand it. Embrace it. It is telling you the problem you're designed to solve and in exercising that solution you will find peace, meaning, fulfillment, happiness and develop the life you're not living. Your frustration will show you.

PART II
THE PROCESS

2.1 The Process

"I have always believed that process is more important than results."

— MS Dhoni

Nothing happens overnight and there is no such thing as an "overnight success." There is only the appearance of an instant transformation from little known to famous or from poor to wealthy. Everything existing in the universe has gone through a process. You are here because you went through the reproductive process. You own a home because you went through the home buying process. You have the strength to move and do because the food you ate has gone through the digestion process. You may not see or understand the process but there is a process.

We are so fixated on the result, our want, that the process is ignored. We are unwilling to accept that no result of any kind is possible without a process. The avoidance of the process brings about frustration, dissatisfaction and disappointment. For decades, the fitness industry has remained a multi-billion-dollar industry by creating ways to circumvent the weight loss process. There's the Atkins diet, the Mediterranean diet, the Biggest Loser program, the Mayo Clinic Diet, Weight Watchers, the Whole Food diet, the MIND Diet, and the list goes on.

These diets and programs succeed for a few weeks or months, then your body communicates the diet or program isn't natural. It can't be sustained. About the time you realize you will not get the result you want, they've come up with a bigger, better, easier diet or program created using the latest research and data. You reach for the credit card and buy this bigger, better, easier program, convinced it will do the trick. After a few weeks, months, you realize this bigger, better, easier diet or program created using the latest research and data isn't getting the results you desire.

You're frustrated and disappointed again. This is the underlying strategy of the fitness industry and billions upon billions of dollars are being made using this strategy.

To keep my body healthy, strong, and at a weight that enables me to be my best, I know I only need to eat healthy, nutrient dense food, exercise, maintain an active lifestyle, and get adequate rest. If I do these things consistently, I never have to be concerned about gaining weight, becoming obese, having diabetes, heart disease, cancer, high blood pressure, gout and so many other weight-related illnesses. The body inherently knows the process of maintaining a state of homeostasis. There is nothing more I need to do. I don't even need to know how my body performs this process. I only need to know there is a process and what part of the process I am responsible for performing. To concern myself with any more is a waste of time and energy.

The financial, real estate, and get rich industries operate similarly to the fitness industry. There are countless programs and systems available that promise you a way to make millions of dollars in 30 days, 6 months, a year and some boast you can be rich overnight. You whip out the credit card and buy the "5 Steps to Wealth Program" or the "Multi-Millionaire Strategy," or the "Flip your House for Profit in 30 days" program. Yes, it's possible, but not probable, you'll increase your income. Like the process of losing weight is ignored, the process of generating wealth is also ignored and the result you desire isn't possible without a process. This cycle of try-fail will repeat until you accept there is a process. You must understand it and adhere to it.

To create the life you are not living, the life you desire, you must accept there is a process. You must understand the process and adhere to it. When you understand and appreciate the process associated with whatever you are seeking to achieve, there is no stress, no anxiety. When you understand all is bound to a process, you know your desired results don't have to be hoped for, they are guaranteed. It's time to learn the process around creating the life you desire.

2.2 Awareness

"To become different from what we are, we must have
some awareness of what we are."

— Eric Hoffer

I walk at a nearby high school in the evenings and on the weekends. I usually crisscross the parking lot several times and walk the track. Without fail, I find pennies, dimes, nickels, and quarters. One day I had been walking for nearly an hour and had found no money. I thought about how often I find money. Just as I was about to head to the parking lot to leave, I looked down and saw a dime. Funny thing is, I had walked over that part of the track at least 30-40 times and hadn't noticed the dime. Why hadn't I seen the dime earlier?

My son had a job at a mall in an affluent part of the city. As a valet he regularly parked expensive, exotic cars. I'm at the mall one day talking to him and a gleaming, black, convertible glides into the valet area. The seats were 100% leather, the dashboard made of genuine wood, stainless steel adorned the interior and door handles. The sound of the engine vibrated through my entire body like I was sitting in a massage chair. I had never looked at a car as more than a means of transportation but this car changed that. I didn't know I could want a car as much as I wanted this car. The imagery and energy were seared into my mind. My son told me the car was a Bentley Continental GT Convertible. I had never seen or heard of this car before. For the next several days I was on YouTube, Facebook, websites that sell exotic cars, and I went to an exotic car dealership to actually see one. A funny thing happened, even though I had never seen one of these cars on the road, in the span of about a month I saw 5. How did I go from having never seen the car before to seeing several in a month?

The dime I found while walking on the track, did it just suddenly appear or was it always there? Did Bentley start making their Continental GT when I saw it for the first time at the mall or were they always being manufactured? The dime was always there and Bentley had been making their Continental GT for over 20 years. I just wasn't aware.

Awareness is the state or ability to perceive, feel, or be conscious of events, objects or sensory patterns. Every human being has awareness. There is nothing you have to *do* to have awareness and there is nothing you cannot become aware of. You have awareness even in the womb. Awareness is the light coming on in a dark room. The items in the room didn't get brought in when the light came on. They were already there. You just weren't aware of them. Awareness is light, illuminating and spotlighting. Once you become aware of something you can never be unaware of that thing just as you cannot unsee what you have seen. Once the light comes on you can never return to the comfort of darkness and ignorance. You are now responsible just as a woman becomes more responsible for her health when she learns she is pregnant. When I became aware that money is all around me all the time, I began to notice it and find it. When I became aware of the Bentley Continental GT, I began to see them.

Awareness is paying attention to something, focusing, and when you pay attention to something, you notice it in a specific, detailed way. If you pay attention to a beautiful woman or a handsome man, you notice the symmetry of her body, his distinct muscle groups, her earrings, the color of her eyes, the number of buttons on his suit jacket, the shape of her face, the color of her hair, how she walks, how he enters the room with confidence. You notice the individual details that make the whole person. Awareness is already upon you. You're reading this book because you know you're struggling with unhappiness and regret in your life. With awareness comes a search for improvement, a solution.

To create the meaningful life, I believe you're obligated to live, you must apply awareness to your thoughts and specifically to your beliefs. Your thoughts and beliefs have carried you to the current place in your life and it is your thoughts and beliefs that will carry you to the life you're not living. You bring awareness to your thoughts by monitoring them. Pay attention to the thoughts, the voice, speaking in your head. Don't judge, just observe your thoughts, as though you were eavesdropping on a private conversation. When you think about, imagine, what your ideal life will look like, do your thoughts empower you or deny you? Do they lift you or tear away at you? Just notice them. Do you hear "you can't do that," "you tried that before and it didn't work," or "that's not a good idea right now."?

As an exercise in awareness, answer these questions. You may know the answers immediately or it may take some thought. It doesn't matter. Answering the questions will create an awareness around what you believe in the area of purpose.

- Do you believe you have a singular purpose?
- Do you believe purpose is something which must be "found?"
- Do you "know" your purpose?
- Is passion the guide to your purpose in life?

I'm not here to tell you what to believe. I intend to identify for you the beliefs that had me living in dissatisfaction and frustration so you can prevent them from holding you in a similar state. Awareness changes your experiences. Your life will no longer be automatic. You will understand and recognize you are the creator of your thoughts and your life. The next step forward awaits you.

2.3 Acknowledgment

"We grow by acknowledging there is an area within ourselves and within our life that can be stronger and re-aligned to our highest good. This acknowledgment requires honesty."

— Victoria L. White

Awareness is very important but alone is not enough to manifest the life you're not living. When you know or learn of something, you inherit a responsibility to act or not act based on what you have become aware of. A simpler way to say this is, once you become aware, you become responsible. Every cell in my body was dissatisfied and frustrated with the state of my life at the time. I was undeniably aware there was more to do and be with my life, yet I did nothing more than be aware of the frustration and dissatisfaction. I was aware and the inherited responsibility was welcomed, yet I didn't act, even though what I had become aware of was a serious benefit. Why didn't I take action when I knew there was a direct benefit? Why did I know better and not do better?

Rape and sexual assault are two extremely, horrendous, acts but the trauma resulting from these acts is exacerbated when the victim isn't believed. The media is filled with instances where a woman has come forth with accusations of being sexually assaulted or raped and she isn't believed or her credibility is questioned. As human beings, we all want to be seen and to be acknowledged. To acknowledge is to accept or admit the existence or truth of. To not acknowledge a crime was committed or a person harmed is to deny the truth. It is the equivalent of saying nothing ever happened. Without acknowledgment, there is no truth, no event, no reality. To not acknowledge a crime is saying no crime was committed so there is nothing to act upon.

Every cell in my body was dissatisfied and frustrated with the state of my life at the time yet I did nothing other than stew in my dissatisfaction and frustration. I didn't take action because I never acknowledged the cause of what was keeping me from the life I desired. There had to be an acknowledgment. Acknowledgment is about honoring your Self. Acknowledgment is about respecting your Self. Acknowledgment is embracing honesty about your life, your circumstances and your situation. By not acknowledging, by not being honest and admitting I was unhappy, dissatisfied, frustrated, empty, I was essentially saying nothing is wrong, all is well as it is, and nothing must change. Why would I take action to change anything when I was embracing the illusion there was nothing wrong? Nothing changes for the sake of change.

To manifest the change required to bring about my best life, I had to acknowledge what I had believed surrounding meaning and purpose in life. Otherwise, those beliefs would go unchallenged and I would continue to be kept away from the life I so desired. You can't move forward if you refuse to acknowledge you're stuck. Have you spent your life believing purpose was something to be found? Have you spent your life believing purpose would be discovered via a passion of yours? Have you spent your life believing you knew your purpose or could know your purpose? Have you spent your life looking for *a* purpose believing you were born to live out some grand singular calling?

This is a moment for personal honesty. You must be willing to acknowledge what is or isn't in your life, what you have and don't have, what you want and don't want. Acknowledge you're not where you want to be in life. Acknowledge it has nothing to do with not working hard enough, not having the right strategy, the 5-step plan, or the 30-day solution. It is your beliefs guiding you and until you acknowledge that truth you will never summit your mountain.

2.4 Assessment

"I made my own assessment of my life, and I began to live it. That was freedom."

— Fernando Flores

Starting my 7th-grade year I was attending my third new school. By the time I graduated from high school my k-12 experience was spent at 8 schools. We moved a lot. To this day I despise moving.

My mother is very organized and neat. She doesn't tolerate clutter and doesn't have the habit of just keeping stuff. One thing I recognized my mother did each time we moved was to determine where we were going and what would best serve us when we got there.

As an adult, I've moved a couple of times and helped others move, and as much as I dislike it, moving provides an opportunity to learn and identify the obstacles in your life. Going into the closets, cabinets, dressers, garage, the basement, all the places that keep your stuff out of sight and pulling stuff out to pack is startling to most people. When I'm helping someone move, about the time they start pulling stuff out to pack, I would hear them say, "Where did all this stuff come from?" as if it just appeared in a cloud of smoke or an elf brought it in. Once they're over the shock of how much stuff they have, the next and most important question I hear is, "What am I going to do with this" or "Should I take this or leave it?"

In the answers to these questions lie the opportunity to learn and identify the obstacles in your life. The overwhelming response is "I'm not sure. Just bring it," or "Keep it. I can find someone to give it to." My mother would always have an answer and it was derived from the question "can this serve me where I'm going?" If yes, it went into a box. If no, it went to the dumpster or to a pile to be donated. I didn't know it at the time but she was demonstrating to me a very important step in creating the life I desired. I was learning how to assess.

Moving is stressful and frustrating but it can become a horror story when it's time to assess. One of the biggest arguments I had with my wife at the time, involved assessment. When moving you must assess what is coming with you and what you will leave behind. You're thinking about where you're going and if it's worth the time, energy and cost to bring along things that aren't going to serve you in your next place. My wife didn't want to part with anything. Everything was coming, regardless if it was used a little or not at all. This is very important. When you're moving to a new station in life, everything you currently possess can't be necessary to bring along. There has to be something that you have grown out of, no longer use or is outdated. If you are bringing *everything* with you, then you as a person haven't grown or evolved. You are making the statement, I am the same person now, that I was when I moved in, however long ago.

This applies to what you believe. When you are desiring to go to a new level in life, to have what you have never had, to do what you have never done, you must leave some beliefs behind. It's not possible to have what you have never had and do what you have never done by adhering to the same beliefs that got you to your current place in life. You're not at the next level because what got you to where you are can't take you to where you want to go. If the beliefs you have could take you to the next level, you would be at the next level already.

When I decided I wanted to do something with my life beyond raising my children, having a good job, paying bills, paying for college, saving for retirement, and taking the average two weeks per year vacation, I had to let go of many things I believed and cherished. Some of what I had to release had been a part of my make-up since childhood. I had to stop believing my path to happiness and fulfillment was to spend 30 years on a job then retire. I had to let go of the belief I had to *find* my purpose in life. I had to release the belief my life was in the hands of someone else. I had to disavow the belief my path in life was pre-determined. I had to lose the belief my passion would lead me to my purpose. I had to toss aside the belief being overweight, having high blood pressure, diabetes, high cholesterol, aches and pains is the norm as you get older. When I made that next move in life, to have the life I wasn't living, I had to stop and make an assessment. I had to ask real, introspective questions. Is this belief going to deliver the life I desire? Can this belief serve me in living my best life? If yes, pack it up. If no, put it in the dump pile.

After years of frustration with your life, you decided to experience a more fulfilling, happy, life. You are ready to live the life you've never had. All your beliefs and hang-ups are spread out in front of you. It is time to assess which beliefs are coming with you and which beliefs are you going to leave behind. Remember, everything can't go with you. There has to be a belief you have grown out of, should no longer trust, or is outdated. This may be difficult because some of what you believe was put into you by your parents and you may feel conflicted as though you're going against them. Some beliefs have been reinforced by society, the media and leadership. This may cause you to feel that by changing or discarding the belief you're a misfit or a weirdo. It's not unusual to feel this way. Understand that your beliefs have been leading you for years, maybe your entire life. They have been in control and won't easily relinquish this control.

When these feelings of conflict and being weird arise, they can guilt you into making decisions that will keep you in the same situation. You're going to need something simple that can keep you focused on what is going to move you forward. For me, I would lean on the foundational question, the question I saw my mother use whenever we were moving from an old space to a new place. I altered the question and it has guided me to my best life, can this belief serve me where I'm going? If yes, pack it up. If no, put it in the dump pile.

Can your current beliefs serve you where you're going? If yes, pack them up. If no, put them in the dump pile.

2.5 Acceptance

"IT happened. There is no avoiding it, no forgetting. No running away, or flying, or burying, or hiding."

— Laurie Halse Anderson

One afternoon while talking with my friend Patty, she got a call from her sister. A broad smile eased across her face and she nodded pleasantly as she chatted. I turned away to watch a rare summer breeze wind through the trees bringing a moment of relief to the humid day. When I turned to Patty again, she was holding the phone away from her as far as her left arm would allow. She stared at the phone wide-eyed as though it had said something offensive to her. Her right hand was covering her mouth and her eyes were getting puffy and watery. I waited for the call to end doing what I could to prepare myself to respond to what I knew was bad news.

Her sister said the man who Patty had known to be her father, who had died several years earlier, was not her father. Her real father was still alive and living somewhere in Georgia. Over fifty years of lies, deception, and complicity had been exercised on her life and she had been completely unaware. Everything she believed, trusted and relied on, was now in doubt. Her entire life, choices, decisions, promises, feelings, expressions, thoughts and ideas were made based on what she had believed, what she had been led to believe about a man who had acted as her father for over fifty years. In a matter of seconds her truth was smashed up and destroyed like a mobile home in the windy grasp of an F5 tornado. How could she ever overcome this upheaval in her life?

I got no phone call but I got a wake-up call in the form of frustration, emptiness, and boredom with my life. After several years of following the thought leaders in purposeful living, reading the top books, and countless articles, everything I believed, trusted and relied on, was now in doubt. I was desperate to have a life of purpose and meaning and I was grudgingly aware of the fact, my life of purpose and meaning would never be a reality with the information and guidance I had been consuming. My beliefs surrounding purpose had not served me and I would have to release them, put them in the dump pile. My problem was I didn't know if I could release them or how to do it.

Patty and I were in a similar situation, we could not move forward in life because of our beliefs. She could not let go of the belief her father wasn't her father and I could not let go of the beliefs, I had to find my purpose, I had *a* purpose, and someday I would know my purpose, along with so many more things I had been led to believe about life and how it should be lived. There was only one way for both of us to be free. We needed to experience acceptance.

The general, dictionary definition of acceptance is the action or process of being received as adequate or suitable. For the context of this book I prefer a more concise definition.

Acceptance is ownership. Acceptance is taking responsibility. Acceptance is taking on as yours, all outcomes, results and consequences. Acceptance is saying I am ready for change and however it appears I will surrender to it. Acceptance means to embrace *what is* without resistance. With acceptance, there is no blame, no shame, no more apologies and no more finger-pointing. There is only calm and peace. True acceptance transforms suffering into ease, pain into love, and emptiness into fulfillment. True acceptance is a form of forgiveness. It is you allowing yourself to be free of what was, to pursue what can be.

Involved in every choice and decision you have ever made was a truth and a belief. When you accept the *truth,* you are free to live completely and abundantly. When you accept the *belief,* you are bound and restricted.

A good example of this is my marriage experience. Friendship, love, trust, compatibility, all the foundational components of a marriage had eroded from abundant to scarce. The belief was you marry for life, I have just one soulmate, if I get divorced, I'm a quitter, society doesn't condone divorce, divorce scars children for life, along with a few others. I would not accept the relationship wasn't serving me anymore. It wasn't serving her anymore and it wasn't serving the children. The relationship had become a hindrance but I still would not accept the truth, it was time to let go. And as long as I refused to accept this truth I suffered in hurt, frustration and anxiety. Instead, I accepted the belief, and for many years it prevented me and the family from a peaceful, caring, loving existence. Suffering was the norm until I accepted divorce as a truth.

This will sound simple, but to experience acceptance, you just must make the decision, be open and be intentional. The decision was difficult for me because it required me to go against so much of what I believed and felt to be the truth. But to have my best life, the life I wasn't living, I had to accept the truth that I am a solution, I will never *know* what I was born to do, I'm not here to do *a* thing, I can create my life, passion is only the beginning, and I must submit to the process. This didn't happen overnight but I stayed with the decision and every day I operated with intent. I paid attention to the choices and decisions I was making and not just major choices and decisions but my daily decisions. Awareness spread and I became more awake to opportunities and people who could help me in experiencing my best life.

Acceptance isn't easy. You may struggle with putting your pride aside or taking responsibility for where you are in life and who you have become. It's not about blame, just own it. Whatever your situation, it was you who put yourself in your current position and it is you who can get yourself out. Your responsibility may not lie in what was done to you. Often, you were a child and unable to assert change or you were an adult and unaware. Your responsibility isn't in what was done but how you respond to what was done. Now that you're ready to own your stuff, it's time to take action.

2.6 Action

"Thinking is easy, acting is difficult, and to put one's thoughts into action is the most difficult thing in the world."

— Johann Wolfgang von Goethe

Every person has a vision or an image of what they want their life to look like. Do you remember, as a child, the vision you had of your life? Do you remember what you imagined your life would look when you were in your 20s? Has your vision changed? Did you give up on the vision or did it no longer fit? Has the vision of your life become a reality?

100% of adults can tell you what their best life looks like. Sadly, 98% of adults will never see the vision of their life manifested. Action has many definitions, but they all have one common factor, movement. When you think of action, you think of motion, movement, doing. Probably the most well-known term or slogan regarding action is *Just Do It*.

Just Do It, the empowering slogan of the Nike corporation verbalizes a mindset the majority of society believes is necessary to be successful. The slogan is wonderful because it is void of hesitation, fear and it empowers action. How can you have a clear image of the life you want yet never see it manifested? Because you don't take action. Most people don't act on the ideas and desires they have. These people make up the 98% I mentioned earlier.

Also, within that 98% is a group that takes action but it's not the actions that will consistently bring about the results they desire. Society has fallen in love with a misguided belief, borderline law, that you always must be doing, going, chasing, grinding, clawing, and scrapping, for what you want in life. *Just Do It* fuels this commonly held belief you always have to be *doing* something. You'll get the "lazy" label if you're not running around like your hair is on fire. You won't be taken seriously if someone asks what you're doing to make your dreams a reality and you can't rattle off at least 10 things you're juggling. Is grinding, chasing, going, and doing necessary to succeed? No, but action-focused and generated from within is necessary. But what is it that determines the *action* you decide to take?

One of the most important things I have discovered recently is I don't make choices, my beliefs do. You don't make choices, your beliefs do. Your entire life you've been taking action based on what you believed about yourself and your surroundings at that time. Everything you've done or didn't do has been based on what you believe. Since your actions are based on what you believe, it is vitally important to have a level of awareness around what you believe before you make a move. You're taking action based on a set of beliefs you have never vetted or challenged to determine if they're serving your best interest. This is why the thinking to Just Do It is so detrimental to manifesting the life you're not living.

The *Just Do It* culture mandates action is the first step in the process when it should always be the last step. Before you ever take action, you should allow awareness to expand in you. Awareness exposes the beliefs and thinking you're cradling that have kept you in your current place and in your comfort zone. Being aware of what is holding you back eliminates the need to grind, chase, scrap and struggle. There is nothing to overcome when you have removed the obstacles.

When you're operating in awareness, with the other steps, your movements and actions are seasoned with clarity and focus. Your steps will have meaning and purpose. When you're operating in Just Do It, or like your hair is on fire, it's impressive to others because they're also under the trance of Just Do It, but you're stressing your body, shortening your life, creating obstacles and increasing the distance between you and your dreams.

I believed the key to having the life I was not living was to find and follow whatever I had a passion for. I believed I had a singular calling. I believed I would someday come to *know* what I was born to do. These are some beliefs that were directing my actions and kept delivering unsatisfactory results and frustrations. I did not understand I was being driven by these beliefs and they were directly responsible for the image of my life not becoming a reality. I had spent a chunk of my life looking for my passion. I had spent a chunk of my life searching for this one thing I was born to do. I had spent a chunk of my life waiting to *know* my reason for being born. What I believed about purpose would never make my dream life come true. I would either drop these beliefs or stop acting on them until I had vetted them and determined if they could carry me to the life I desired.

So, if you believe you have a sole purpose in life, you will never notice the other hundred incredible opportunities available for you to have breathtaking experiences. If you believe you *know* your reason for being born, you will be blind to what else your talents will allow you to fall in love with and master. If you believe life is to be discovered, you will always be led to and through your life and never leading. You will always be under someone's charge and never in charge. If you're not getting the results you want, then stop. Be still. It's alright to not do anything. Frustration and dissatisfaction are incredible indicators that a pause and assessment must be done, and a change implemented.

Instead of always taking physical action, you need to take mental action. This is always the best approach. In your mind is where everything begins. Challenge your beliefs and determine if they can still serve you and deliver the life you desire. Do the trial and error in your imagination. Allow your mind to be the laboratory, exercise it there, test it there, envision it there. What would your life look like if you started creating your life instead of discovering it? What would your life look like if you lived with a purpose instead of living for a purpose? How would your life change if you never knew what you were on this Earth to do? You can ask and answer these questions in your mind with no cost or fear of making a mistake.

Action should be the last step in this wonderful process to have the life you're not living. For all that is created, there is a process, and if you follow the process, all that you desire to create will become your reality.

ERIC THOMAS

2.7 Last Thoughts

"The fear of death follows from the fear of life. The one who lives fully is prepared to die at any time."

— Mark Twain

I have no idea when it will happen but it will happen to me, and it will happen to you. Death. It is our inevitable, common denominator.

Since death is guaranteed and I have no clue when it will appear, I decided not to spend more than the time needed to plan my departure or thinking about it. That decision has allowed me to spend an enormous amount of time on what matters, living. And not just living but living the best life imaginable. I want to experience a happy, meaningful, joyous, impactful, and healthy, life. A life my children can use as a template for how they would like to design their life. To accomplish this, I had to release who I believed myself to be.

You are solely responsible for the experiences in your life and it is your obligation to experience all that you desire. To have the life you're not living, you too must release who you *believe* yourself to be.

The person you are now is not your true Self. The person you are now was created based on who you were instructed to be, by your parents, teachers, friends, family, the media. Their instructions became your beliefs which became the building material, the steel, the concrete, you. Now is the time to implode this person, the current you, so you can create the true you based on how *you* feel and what *you* believe. Ask your Self, who do I want to become? What do I want to experience? Create your life with the answers to these questions, the feelings and intuitions from your Self. Allow them to become your Sherpa.

If you create your life from your feelings, your intuition, and your desires, you will have a life that exceeds a simple search for purpose and meaning. You will have a life that manifests your true purpose, to live a life according to You.

LEAVE ME A REVIEW!

Thank you for reading the book. Reviews are very important. Please take a moment to leave a review on Amazon or wherever you purchased the book. I'm always interested to know what you like, think and want. I personally read every review.

ABOUT THE AUTHOR

Eric Thomas is a full-time author, blogger, and Transformational Speaker. Having spent over ten years searching for his purpose, reading hundreds of self-help books with antiquated ideas that just left him going around in circles, Eric discovered the importance of changing your mindset and the way you see the world. Now, his goal is to teach people the lessons he learned through trial-and-error, helping them find their purpose, stop feeling aimless, and live their best possible lives.

Visit ThePurposeMap.com

Made in the USA
Columbia, SC
11 February 2020